MOLLY'S GREATEST ESCAPE
A Little Story about a Small Octopus

Written and Illustrated by Diane Moody
Copyright 2011

For Molly (Mollusk) Octopus and all the octopuses in the oceans.

The sunlight filters down through the clear cool water as Molly moves along the ocean floor looking for food.

Her world is huge and filled with beauty.

Sea creatures of every size and shape show off their amazing colors. Seagrasses and seaweed dance to the rhythm of the waves.

But, for a small octopus, it is very dangerous. She never knows where danger may be lurking. She uses the skills she was born with to escape predators. Moving toward a pile of rocks, she spots a movement.

"Is it danger or a tasty snack?" wonders Molly. Cautiously, she moves toward the rocks.

"This looks like a great place to find my next meal."

Suddenly, an eel darts out of the rocks! Its mouth is full of razor-sharp teeth that just miss Molly as she jets toward a small crevice in the rocks. Because she has no bones, she easily squeezes into a tiny crack.

"He can't get me now," laughs Molly.

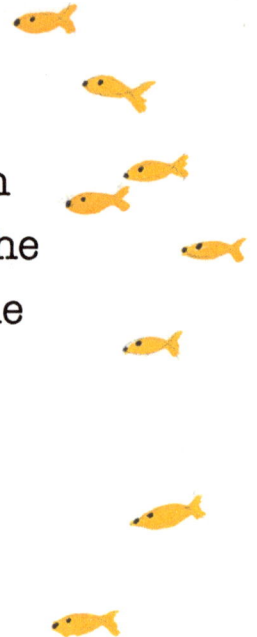

Once inside the rocks, Molly can't see the eel.

"Luckily I can stick my eyes above the
rocks to see if he's still here."

When she is sure the eel has gone, she continues her search for
food. Molly soon finds a bed of oysters. Using her sharp beak and
powerful suction cups, she opens the shells and eats her dinner.

"Mmmm, mmmm, mmmm! That was delicious.
Now I can go home to my cave."

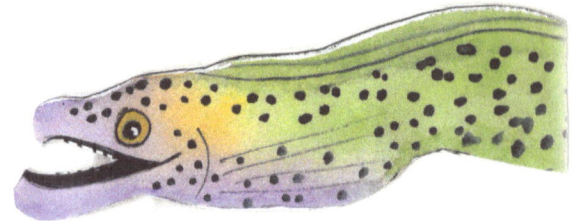

As she leaves her cave the next morning, Molly is hungry again. Dreaming of juicy morsels, clams, oysters, and maybe a scallop or two, she ventures out and begins her search.

A stingray slowly glides above the sand as little seahorses dart around in the seaweed. A school of brightly-colored fish swim in the distance.

Enjoying all the beauty, Molly slowly moves on.

Without warning, a large shadow falls over her!
A school of barracuda dives toward her at lightning
speed! She silently drops to the ocean floor and changes
her color and her texture to match the sandy bottom.

"Whew! That was close. Without a clever trick
like that, I'd be a goner," sighs Molly.

"Now if I don't move, I'll be invisible.
Besides, I can always use a little nap."

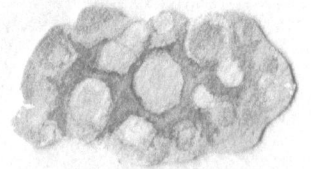

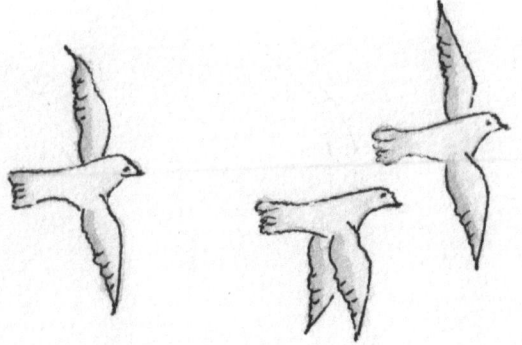

After they leave, Molly moves closer to the shore.
She finds a rocky outcropping and a tide pool full of all kinds of
delicious things to eat. She takes her time exploring the pool.

She doesn't worry when the tide goes out, because
pools of water are left among the rocks. When the tide
comes back in, she knows she can return to the ocean.

Molly continues
searching the tide
pool and spots some
clams. As she moves
toward them, she
sees a movement
above the water.
It's Ben. His family is vacationing at the beach.
Ben loves to walk along the sandy shore looking for
shells. Near a pile of rocks, he spots the tide pool.

He knows tide pools are great places to explore because
they are full of all kinds of interesting sea creatures.

"Wow!" Ben whispers when he sees the little octopus.
"You are so awesome! I know why you are called octopus.
Octo means eight and you have eight arms."

Ben puts his hand in the water. Molly, the little octopus, cautiously watches him. She is very shy, but finally her curiosity gets the best of her. Molly moves close enough to touch his hand. Realizing she isn't in any danger, she uses several of her arms to investigate Ben's hand and fingers.

"Oh! You want to be my friend," whispers Ben. "I've never had a friend like you."

After playing a while, Ben says, "I have to go now, but I'll be back tomorrow. Sure hope you'll be here."

Molly returns to her cave when the tide comes back in.

The next day, Molly heads for the rocky shore. She remembers the good hunting. In a hurry to find her next meal, she doesn't see the seal coming straight for her at top speed. It gets closer, closer, closer! Sensing danger, she quickly squirts her ink and jet propels away. The seal can't see or smell the direction of her escape.

"That was soooo close! I guess I'd better pay attention to what's going on around me," Molly scolds herself. Carefully, she continues on to the tide pool.

Ben goes straight to the tide pool
when he returns to the beach.

"I wonder if she'll be there today.
Yes! She came back!" he cries when he spots her.

Ben is fascinated as he watches Molly open and eat clams
and mussels. He remembers a trip to the aquarium, where he
learned octopuses are not only curious but very intelligent.
They can solve a problem and remember how to do it again.

When Molly moves close enough, Ben touches
her skin and she turns a rainbow of colors.

"That's so cool!" says Ben. "You're magical. I can't
wait to come back tomorrow so we can play again!"

When the tide comes back in,
Molly leaves the tide pool and heads home.
She sees some beautiful jellyfish that seem
to be floating along with the current.

"Gosh, one of the jellyfish is being
left behind," thinks Molly.

But it isn't a jellyfish. Molly has
never seen anything like it.

Curious, she moves closer.

As Molly puts out an arm to touch it, the current carries it over her. It's a bag, a PLASTIC bag, and she is covered by it. She frantically tries to push it away.

"What is happening? Why can't I get away from it?" cries Molly.

The more she struggles, the tighter it wraps around her. She can't swim. She is at the mercy of the waves—bobbing along in the current until she is finally washed ashore.

Exhausted from trying to get out of the bag, Molly lies on the beach—TRAPPED.

"Boy, am I in trouble now. I don't know how to escape from this," gasps Molly.

When Ben returns to the tide pool, he's very disappointed Molly isn't there.

"Where are you today?" he asks out loud. "Maybe you're in another pool."

As he searches, he picks up trash left on the beach by careless people. He had seen a video at the aquarium explaining how trash is causing harm and injury to sea creatures. He reaches for a plastic bag and sees it move. Looking inside, he is very surprised to see Molly.

"I didn't know where you were!" shouts Ben. "I'm so glad I found you. You're very special."

Ben takes Molly out of the bag and puts
her in the water. He watches as the waves
slowly carry her back into the ocean.

"I'll look for you again tomorrow. I hope
you'll come back and play," calls Ben.
"You are my very special friend."

As Molly returns to her life in the sea
she thinks, "I'm so happy you helped me
escape. Now I CAN come back and play."

# AMAZING OCTOPUS FACTS

Octopuses do not learn from their parents. They inherit their physical abilities and instincts.

Octopuses don't have any bones, so they can squeeze into very small openings.
A sixty-pound Giant Pacific Octopus got through a two-inch opening in an aquarium.

Octopuses can raise their eyes above their heads and turn them 180 degrees.
They can look behind themselves without turning around.

Octopuses can change the color and texture of their skin in two-thirds of a second to imitate the color and texture of sand or rock.

Octopuses live alone, are very shy, but also very curious. They are considered one of the smartest animals in the ocean.

When threatened, the octopus can squirt ink that blinds the predator and masks the smell of the octopus. Then, it can jet away.

When a diver touches an octopus, they sometimes turn a rainbow of colors.

An octopus can lose an arm to a predator and it will grow back.

The octopus has a well-developed nervous system, brain and eyes. It can solve problems like figuring out how to open a jar, and it remembers what it has learned.

There are about 150 kinds of octopuses
living in the oceans around the world.
Most are one to two feet long.

# TERRIBLE TRASH FACTS

### Trash is causing injuries and death to sea animals.

## There are many ways trash gets into the ocean:

**PEOPLE** leave their trash on the beach; plastic containers, plastic bags, party balloons, beach toys, broken bottles, metal cans. When the tide goes out, the waves carry it into the ocean.

**BOATS** throw all kinds of trash and old fishing gear into the ocean.

**OIL BARGES** have accidental leaks and spills, and clean their waste tanks at sea.

## These are some of the ways trash causes harm:

Thousands of sea birds get tangled in fishing nets and lines. They get covered with oil from spills and leaks.

Turtles, seals, and many other animals
swallow plastic bags that look like jellyfish.

Plastic breaks down into tiny pieces as small as plankton.
Many animals, including whales, swallow it.

### THE TRASH IN THE OCEAN
### NEVER COMPLETELY GOES AWAY.

www.ingramcontent.com/pod-product-compliance
Lightning Source LLC
Chambersburg PA
CBHW041239040426
42445CB00004B/83